OBSERVING NATURE

Duck

Written by Stephen Savage

Illustrated by Stephen Lings

Thomson Learning
New York

OBSERVING NATURE

Ant   Duck

Butterfly   Frog

First published in the
United States in 1995 by
Thomson Learning
115 Fifth Avenue
New York, NY 10003

Published simultaneously in
Great Britain by
Wayland (Publishers) Ltd.

Library of Congress Cataloging-in-
Publication Data
Savage, Stephen, 1965–
  Duck / written by Stephen Savage;
illustrated by Stephen Lings.
      p.   cm.—(Observing nature)
  Includes index.
  ISBN 1-56847-328-1
  1. Mallard—Juvenile literature.
2. Mallard—Life cycles—Juvenile
literature. [1. Mallard. 2. Ducks] I. Lings,
Stephen, ill. II. Title. III. Series: Savage,
Stephen, 1956– Observing nature.
QL696.A52S28   1995
598.4'1—dc20   94-39371

Printed in Italy

Contents

What Is a Mallard?

If you visit a large pond or lake, you will probably see mallard ducks. Like all ducks, mallards have waterproof feathers that help them to float. Their webbed feet are like paddles that help them to swim. They can even walk on soft mud without sinking.

Mallards that live
near towns are often
tame. They will eat bread that
you throw to them, and some will
eat from your hand.

The Male Mallard

The male mallard, called a drake, is more colorful than the female. His bright colored feathers will help him attract a mate. The male mallard will molt his feathers in the summer. His new feathers will be brown like the female's.

6

The mallard has a flat beak for feeding on small water creatures. Sometimes mallards catch food at the bottoms of ponds.

When they dive, only their tails can be seen.

The Female Mallard

Male and female mallard ducks look very different. The female mallard, called a hen, is brown, a good color for hiding from danger. You will often see mallard ducks asleep on the edge of a pond. This is because they usually feed at night. They also spend a lot of time preening their feathers.

Mallards do not always feed near water. They sometimes feed in fields and even woodlands. There they eat worms, insects, and acorns.

In Air and Water

On the ground, a mallard walks with a slow waddle.
In the sky, they are strong, fast fliers. Mallards often
land on water. As they come into land, they open
their wings to slow down. The ducks land on the
water feet first, spraying water
into the air.

Some mallards migrate from areas where the winter is very cold. They fly for very long distances to reach places where the winter weather is warmer.

Making a Nest

In the spring, the male mallard attracts a female by doing a special dance. He fluffs up his feathers, waggles his tail, and nods his head up and down.

The nest is often built in long grass, a short distance from water. The male mallard chooses a safe place to build it. Only the female makes the nest, using grasses and dead leaves. Sometimes this may be built high up in a hole in a tree!

Laying the Eggs

The female mallard covers the
bottom of the nest with a layer of
soft, downy feathers. In March
she will lay her green-brown
eggs. This mallard has laid nine
eggs. The female sits on the eggs
to keep them warm and to hide
them from danger.

The female sits very still so that she will not be seen. If she has to leave the nest, she will cover the eggs with the downy feathers.

Inside the Eggs

The baby mallards grow safely inside the eggs. The yellow part inside the egg is the yolk. This is the baby duck's food until it hatches out of the egg.

The female mallard will sit on the eggs until they hatch. After three and a half weeks, the nine mallard chicks will have grown too big for the eggs. Now they are ready to hatch.

The Eggs Hatch

The baby ducks peck their way out of the eggs. The newly hatched ducklings are tired and wet. Their eyes are already open, and soon their feathers are dry and fluffy.

A few hours after they hatch, the ducklings are running around and looking for food. There are many dangers, so the chicks stay close to their mother for safety.

Feeding

The ducklings peck at the ground and grass as they look for food. Although they can feed themselves, they do not know what is good to eat. The mother duck will lead the chicks to places where food can be found.

The young ducklings learn to eat all sorts of food. They will eat insects, snails, and small pieces of green plants.

Swimming

After two days, the ducklings are led to water for their first swim. The mother duck keeps the ducklings close to her at all times. Some ducks have to lead their chicks across busy roads before they reach water.

Some of the ducklings
are unwilling to go in the
water at first. The cold water feels
strange to them. The mother calls the ducklings,
and soon they are all swimming along behind her.

Dangers

The ducklings may face danger from land, air, or water. Foxes, stoats, cats, birds of prey, and even some large fish may attack ducklings. The mother duck may try to lure the attacker away by pretending to be hurt.

The ducklings scatter and hide in the grass or they dive into the water. The color of the chicks' feathers helps them to hide from danger. Mallards can be poisoned if they accidentally eat small lead fishing weights that have been left behind by careless fishermen.

Grown Up

The ducklings spend more time away from their mother as they explore the pond on their own. Now the young ducks are two months old and they are old enough to fly.

The young ducks can now look after themselves.

Very soon, they will fly away to find

another pond where they can live.

Other Water Birds

There are many other water birds that live on ponds and rivers. The shy Florida gallinule, or moorhen, has large feet that are good for walking on lily pads. The graceful swan is easy to recognize with its long neck and pure white feathers.

swallows

pintail ducks

moorhen

Some geese look like
swans, but they have
shorter necks and make a
noisy honking sound. You
may also see other types of
ducks and small birds
that have come to the pond
to drink.

graylag geese

mute swan

swallow

Life of a Duck

1 The male mallard

2 The female mallard

3 In air and water

4 Making a nest

5 Laying the eggs

6 Inside the eggs

7 The eggs hatch

8 Feeding

9 Swimming

10 Dangers

11 All grown up

Glossary

attack To try to kill something.

attract To make something want to come near you.

lure To attract attention by tricking.

migrate To go from one area or country to another, at certain times of year.

molt To lose feathers.

preening A bird's cleaning of its feathers by using its beak.

tame Not afraid of people.

Index